Nancy Lee
          Feb. 14, 1977

With all my love

Gary.

A Lifetime Filled With Love

A Lifetime Filled With Love

Celebrations of Romance All Through Our Lives

Edited by Tina Hacker

♕ Hallmark Crown Editions

The publisher wishes to thank those who have given their kind permission to reprint material included in this book. Every effort has been made to give proper acknowledgments. Any omissions or errors are deeply regretted, and the publisher, upon notification, will be pleased to make necessary corrections in subsequent editions.

ACKNOWLEDGMENTS: "The Most Beautiful Girl in the World" by Florence Jane Soman. Copyright © 1972 by The Hearst Corporation. Reprinted by permission of Brandt & Brandt. "Afterwards" from *The Heart of Home* by Anne Campbell. Reprinted by permission of the author. "After Two Years" from *The Poems of Richard Aldington* by Richard Aldington. Copyright 1928, 1930, 1933, 1934 by Doubleday & Company, Inc. Reprinted by permission of Doubleday & Company, Inc. "First Date" by Ralph Flanagan from the June, 1951 issue of *Ladies' Home Journal.* © June, 1951 Downe Publishing, Inc. Reprinted with permission of *Ladies' Home Journal.* "Letter About Love" by Paul Engle. Reprinted by permission of the author. "Helpmate" by Georgie Starbuck Galbraith from the February, 1971 issue of *Good Housekeeping.* © 1971 by The Hearst Corporation. Reprinted by permission of the author. "Marriage" by Wilfrid Wilson Gibson. Reprinted by permission of Michael Gibson. "Lover's Lament" by Leonhard Dowty reprinted by permission from the June, 1972 issue of *Good Housekeeping.* © 1972 by The Hearst Corporation. "For a Wedding Anniversary" by Roselle Mercier Montgomery from *The Treasure Chest.* Reprinted by permission of Harper & Row, Publishers. "Married Love" from *How Love Grows in Marriage* by Leland Foster Wood. Copyright 1950 by Leland Foster Wood. Reprinted by permission of Hawthorn Books, Inc. "Love" by Frederico Velasquez from *Let Them Write Poetry* by Nina Willis Walter. Copyright © 1962 by Holt, Rinehart and Winston, Publishers. Reprinted by permission of Holt, Rinehart and Winston, Publishers. Excerpt reprinted from *The Prophet,* by Kahlil Gibran, with permission of the publisher, Alfred A. Knopf, Inc. Copyright 1923 by Kahlil Gibran; renewal copyright 1951 by Administrators C.T.A. of Kahlil Gibran Estate and Mary G. Gibran. "Poem in Prose" by Archibald MacLeish. Copyright 1948 by Archibald MacLeish. Reprinted from *Actfive and Other Poems,* by Archibald MacLeish, by permission of Random House, Inc. "In Love" and "These Things" from *In Love* by Gordon Parks. Copyright © 1971 by Gordon Parks. Reprinted by permission of J. B. Lippincott Company. "Collar Holler" by Janice Marshall from the July, 1972 issue of *Good Housekeeping.* © 1972 by The Hearst Corporation. Reprinted by permission of the author. "A Decade" from *The Complete Poetical Works of Amy Lowell* by Amy Lowell. Published by Houghton Mifflin Company, and reprinted with their permission. "Speaking of Love" by G. Groman from the June, 1970 issue of *Harvest Years.* Reprinted by permission of *Retirement Living* magazine. "For Those Who Love" from *The Poems of Henry van Dyke* is reprinted by permission of Charles Scribner's Sons. Copyright 1911 by Charles Scribner's Sons. "I Am a Little Child" reprinted by permission from *UNICEF Book of Children's Poems* by William Kaufman, published by Stackpole Books. Copyright 1970 by Stackpole Books. "Then" by William Stafford from the June, 1951 issue of *Ladies' Home Journal.* Copyright © 1975 by William Stafford. Reprinted by permission of the author. Excerpt by James Thurber from the March 14, 1960 issue of *Life* Magazine. Copyright © 1960 Time Inc. Reprinted with permission of the publisher. "Your Voice" from *Your Voice Makes My Knees Tickle!* by Todd Richards. Copyright 1972 by Valley of the Sun Publishing Co. Reprinted with permission. "Young Love" by Theodosia Garrison and "Conversational" from *A Book of Love Poems,* edited by William Cole. Published by The Viking Press, Inc. "You and Me Makes We" by Margie Whelan reprinted by permission from *American Girl,* a magazine for all girls, published monthly by Girl Scouts of the U.S.A. "My Love for You" from *A Diller, A Dollar* by Lillian Morrison. Copyright © 1955 by Lillian Morrison. Reprinted with permission of Thomas Y. Crowell Company, Inc.

PHOTOGRAPHS: Ken Biggs, page 62; Jacqueline Casey, page 8; Larry Couzins, front dust jacket, page 49; Jim Cozad, page 46; Phoebe Dunn, page 59; John Eagan, pages 6-7; Harv Gariety, front dust jacket, pages 20, 60; Elizabeth Gee, pages 19, 35, 42; Carol Hale, page 3; David Hamilton, page 13; Maxine Jacobs, pages 26-27, 32; Elyse Lewin, pages 10-11, Rick Lyons, pages 12, 29, 41, 44-45; Jane McClelland, back dust jacket, page 4; Mike McClue, pages 22, 23, 36; Photo Media, pages 14-15; Bob Segura, title page, pages 16, 24, 30; Ed Simpson, back dust jacket, pages 50-51, 56-57.

Designed by William Hunt.
Set in Gill Sans, a typeface designed by Eric Gill in 1928.
Printed on Hallmark Crown Royale Book paper.

Welcome to
A Lifetime Filled With Love

*Love is the emotion that makes life worth living. It's
that special feeling deep inside that makes us look
forward to each day. When we're in love, jokes seem
wittier, chores seem easier and the sun seems to shine
more often. Ordinary events become fascinating tidbits
to share. Everyday places become filled with memories.
Romance covers every aspect of our lives with a warm glow,
beginning, perhaps, with our first valentine in kindergarten
and continuing undimmed throughout all our years.*

    A Lifetime Filled With Love *explores loving
relationships between people — from love as a
child to love as a mature adult. Here a husband tenderly
explains how much he cherishes his wife after many
years of marriage; a teenage girl writes humorously of
the boy of her dreams; and a child gives us a delightful
picture of romance in grade school. In this book,
young and old alike share their experiences and views
of that wonderful, ever-changing, ever-deepening force
that makes the world go round — love.*

Sometimes it's hard to remember those first flutterings of love. But they were there. Even before we knew it, we were head over heels in love with the boy or girl next door. And more often than not, when we tried to think of just the right thing to say, the opposite came out! Romance was very real when we were young, even if it didn't last longer than a grade or two. As the following selections show, love when we're little is a funny, happy, sad, ecstatic experience that we can never really forget.

My Love for You
By a school child

I love you little, I love you lots;
My love for you would fill ten pots,
Fifteen buckets, sixteen cans,
Three teacups and four dishpans.

I Am a Little Child
By a first grader

I am a little child
   Clean as a little duck.
My ears are all washed,
   My nails and hair are cut.

The whole day in school
   With my bookbag always near
I run, I play and jump
   And I love my teacher dear.

The Shy Valentine

Barbara Burrow

Keep quiet, Willy,
Stop giggling so!
She's sure to hear you,
Then she'll know!
Where's her Valentine?
That's the one.
We'll slip it under the door
          ...and run!

Lover's Lament

Leonhard Dowty

That summer was the summer of Anne,
As blonde as wheat,
Brown-eyed, sweet,
Laughter-filled, 18 and tan,
A girl to turn the heart of any man.
And turn my heart she did, she did.
It flipped and flopped.
It nearly stopped.
But when I made my smitten bid,
Within my chest I heard it skid.
"Too young, too young," was her reply.
I shook my head.
My heart played dead.
Ice and sleet invaded July.
Too young for love, too old to cry.
So there I stood — disqualified —
When I was ten and the world too wide.

Bobby socks, raccoon coats, wearing "his" letter sweater
— the life of today's teenager is no longer occupied
with these. But now, as always, the teen's days are
filled with romance. All the intensity of a lifetime
is squeezed into the teen years — or so it seems. This
is the age when mementoes and promises of undying
devotion are exchanged weekly. And the love that
thrilled us by showing a flair for tennis is soon
replaced by one who is a whiz at math. The modern
knight is most likely wearing blue jeans, and as for
the princess, she's probably playing football.

Conversational
Anonymous

"How's your father?" came the whisper,
    Bashful Ned the silence breaking;
"Oh, he's nicely," Annie murmured,
    Smilingly the question taking.

 Conversation flagged a moment,
    Hopeless Ned essayed another:
"Annie, I — I," then a coughing,
    And the question, "How's your mother?"

"Mother? Oh, she's doing finely!"
    Fleeting fast was all forbearance,
When in low, despairing accents,
    Came the climax, "How's your parents?"

Love
Frederico Velasquez, age 15

How much do I love you?
I cannot say.
Why, why is it,
When I see you coming,
I turn and go the other way?

First Date

Ralph Flanagan

The best time I ever had on a date was on the day that
the New York World's Fair closed for good. I was a
small-town boy playing the piano in Sammy Kaye's orchestra,
and it was my first date with a beautiful model
from Brooklyn. We visited every exhibit, every monument
and curiosity in the fairgrounds and I have one complete
photo album to show for that memorable day. In
fact, I have more than that to show. I married the girl.

Young Love

Theodosia Garrison

Within my bed, the whole night thru,
I turn and turn . . . and think of you;
And wonder, when we met today,
If you said what you meant to say.
And what you thought I thought you meant
And were you sorry when I went;
And did you get my meaning when . . . .
And then the whole thing through again!
I only hope that somewhere you
Are sleeping badly too!

Going Together
Thea Peterson

When he asked me
if we could go steady,
my mind raced back
to all those times
I had said
dating one person only
was silly,
kid stuff,
outdated.
But that was before
I met him,
and answered,
"Of course."

from **Romeo and Juliet**
William Shakespeare

My bounty is as boundless as the sea,
My love as deep; the more I give to thee,
The more I have, for both are infinite.

You and Me Makes We

Margie Whelan, age 16

You were my prince upon your great white horse
Or should I say motorcycle

You were my knight in shining armor
Or should I say jeans

You were my chef who served me seven courses
Or should I say hamburgers

You were always on time when we had a date
Or should I say a little late

But you loved me
Or should I say I thought

When you said good-bye, it was good-bye

Or should I say I thought

But you came back into my life
And now when we have a date
You are a little less late.

Most of us remember the first time we met that very unique someone — the person we'd been waiting for all our lives (or a month or two anyway). It may not have been a glamorous encounter, like finding each other in a rainstorm or discovering we both had a passion for Garbo films. But soon afterwards, there was no doubt — this love was going to be something special.

Before and Ever After

Edward Cunningham

I remember a January
    with someone who liked Baudelaire
       and hot spiced wine,
Yes, and a July with someone else
    whose dearest pleasures were
       drive-in movies and ice-cold beer,
Then, let's see, there was an April
    when I played
       The Sensuous Tennis Instructor,
Not to mention, a September
    when someone kept me dancing
       to the cast album of *Hair*,
But most of all,
    I remember wishing
      there were someone
        who could fill
   all the seasons of my life
    with love,
And when you finally arrived
   believe me
     I was ready.

I'll Remember

Naomi Sheldon

I'll remember the night
I first saw you, when you
had to leave with the girl
but came back to say,
"How can I reach you?"

In Love

Gordon Parks

Slowly down this grimy street I drift
            lovestruck, dream-hung,
Accepting the jeweled mist
To cool my blazing soul,
Hugging the sight of you blowing
            from that unfriendly taxi
Your first handkiss to me.
You are gone and I am empty;
Yet I am full of you —
            of
Something more than I knew
An unpracticed heart could hold.

Afterwards

Anne Campbell

Afterwards it is not the kiss we remember —
Only that one day in gold September
Your spirit met my spirit, and we clung
Together — wordless for one moment, hung
In space . . . . Afterwards recalling — not the greeting,
And not the kiss . . . but just our spirits meeting!

Your Voice
Todd Richards

When your
voice is soft
it makes
my knees tickle.

In the Spring
Alfred, Lord Tennyson

In the Spring a fuller crimson comes upon the robin's breast;
In the Spring the wanton lapwing gets himself another crest;

In the Spring a livelier iris changes on the burnish'd dove;
In the Spring a young man's fancy lightly turns to thoughts of love.

Twentieth-Century Rendezvous
Hadin Marshal

We didn't exactly race
slow motion
through fields of waving wildflowers
in soft focus
and evaporate
into a lyrical kiss,
but somehow
in the middle of a crowded terminal,
despite two leaden Samsonites
and four weary feet,
we struggled together
and were
god so glad
to see each other.

Acting Silly
Julia Summers

Sometimes you're silly.
You act like a little boy
instead of a grown man:
guess-whoing me
with your hands over my eyes,
leaving love notes
under pillows and inside books,
running away from me
and laughing
whenever I act silly
and chase you like a little girl
instead of a grown woman
who is very much in love.

Whether she's wearing a gown of lace or a frock of muslin, whether she walks down an aisle or stands under a cathedral of trees, every bride is a vision of beauty with stars in her eyes. And the groom, standing proudly beside her, knows he has found the most wonderful woman in the world.

For Every Bride

Dixie Willson

For every bride who walks with shining faith
Into the day new promise has begun,
I'd ask not castles reaching to the sun
Nor golden doors to smug security,
But only this...
May love have kept for her,
When twenty other years have come and gone,
The wonder of the rose and purple dawn,
The thrill in every bud that heralds spring,
The peace of evening lights in twilight skies,
The joy of rain upon the thirsty grass...
And dreams to challenge all the years that pass
To dim that star today lights in her eyes.

Marriage

Wilfrid Wilson Gibson

Going my way of old,
Contented more or less,
I dreamt not life could hold
Such happiness.

I dreamt not that love's way
Could keep the golden height,
Day after happy day,
Night after night.

Married Love
Leland Foster Wood

Married living needs the continuance of the dash and
sparkle of romantic love. But the relation of romantic
love to married love is somewhat like that of a little
tree to the larger tree which it later becomes. It has
life and fresh young energy that enables it to grow.
When it has grown into a larger tree, its heart and
vitality are still there but, with continued life, it
has taken new rings of growth, its branches have spread
wider and its roots have gone deeper. Moreover, it
bears flowers and fruit which the little tree did not
produce.

Married love is love woven into a pattern of living.
It has in it the elements of understanding and of the
passionate kindness of husband and wife toward each
other. It is rich in the many-sided joys of life because
each is more concerned with giving joy than with grasping
it for himself. And joys are most truly experienced
when they are most fully shared.

To My Dear and Loving Husband

Anne Bradstreet

If ever two were one, then surely we.
If ever man were lov'd by wife, then thee.
If ever wife was happy in a man,
Compare with me, ye women, if you can.
I prize thy love more than whole mines of gold,
Or all the riches that the East doth hold.
My love is such that rivers cannot quench,
Nor aught but love from thee give recompense.
Thy love is such I can no way repay;
The heavens reward thee manifold I pray.
Then while we live, in love let's so persevere,
That when we live no more, we may live ever.

from **The Prophet**

Kahlil Gibran

Then Almitra spoke again and said, And
 what of Marriage, master?
And he answered saying:
You were born together, and together you
 shall be forevermore.
You shall be together when the white
 wings of death scatter your days.
Aye, you shall be together even in the silent memory
 of God.
But let there be spaces in your togetherness,
And let the winds of the heavens dance between you.

Love one another, but make not a bond of love:
Let it rather be a moving sea between the shores of
 your souls.
Fill each other's cup but drink not from one cup.
Give one another of your bread but eat not from the
 same loaf.
Sing and dance together and be joyous, but let each one
 of you be alone,
Even as the strings of a lute are alone though they
 quiver with the same music.
Give your hearts, but not into each other's keeping.
For only the hand of Life can contain your hearts.
And stand together yet not too near together:
For the pillars of the temple stand apart,
And the oak tree and the cypress grow not in each
 other's shadow.

Ah — the first years of marriage — dreams-come-true
and drains that clog, bliss and a budget, and discovering
that sometimes the state of the laundry is at least as
important as the state of the nation. These years are
a time when love deepens and matures, when we learn
from each other. These are precious years in our
lifetime filled with love.

After Two Years

Richard Aldington

She is all so slight
And tender and white
As a May morning.
She walks without hood
At dusk. It is good
To hear her sing.

It is God's will
That I shall love her still
As He loved Mary,
And night and day
I will go forth to pray
That she love me.

Helpmate
Georgie Starbuck Galbraith

Love did not end my troubles:
I still must fuss and fret,
With silent fear and sorrow,
I bear them even yet.

But love has made me stronger:
I walk the daily road
And with love's arm to brace me,
I scarcely note the load.

Then
William Stafford

I will call you by your softest name.
    Though snow will fall along the farthest hill
Winter will end. Nothing will be the same.
    At first we will not know; and then we will.

Down all the long unceasing breath of day,
    Into our eyes and gently on the land,
The snow will say its whiteness, and I'll say
    Your softest name, your hand within my hand.

7 A.M.
Dean Walley

The first time you saw
my early-morning face,
rumpled, wrinkled, whiskered,
I thought the whole thing was over.
But then you kissed me,
soft as sun through fog,
and I knew that the whole thing
had just begun.

*Although generations
of poets have told us that
a mother-to-be is the most
beautiful woman in the world,
sometimes it's hard
to convince the mother herself.
In the following story,
Kate discovers that beauty
is, indeed, in the beholder's
eye — especially when his
eyes are filled with love.*

The Most Beautiful Girl in the World

Florence Jane Soman

Kate was intrigued almost at once by the new tenant
down the hall. She passed the girl's apartment every
night going to the incinerator, wearing her loose robe
that could not conceal her seven-month pregnancy. She
had taken over this small nightly task since the girl's
arrival, telling Joe that she wanted to "move around a
little after dinner." But the truth was that she liked
to walk slowly past 17C because such lovely sounds came
from there at that hour — languorous cocktail music, the
clink of glasses, soft laughter. Sometimes the elevator
would arrive and some handsome young man would cross
the carpeted hall and ring the bell. The door would
open, then, revealing the girl — a tall blonde with
marvelous legs and a burnished tan, so beautiful in her
little slink of soft dress.

"She makes me feel so ticky-tacky," Kate sighed one
night to Joe, who was reading in his easy chair.

"Who?" He was 30, wore glasses, and was good-looking

in a bookish, slightly disheveled way.

"The new girl down the hall."

He looked up. "Miss Ilona Graham. Yes, she's quite a parcel."

"You know her name?"

"Her mail's still on her doormat when I leave in the morning."

"Why, you old snoop!" She laughed. "She's in the fashion business, the doorman told me." Her agreeably snub-nosed face became pensive. "She's so glamorous!"

His expression grew thoughtful. "Hey, you're not jealous, are you? Because that would be silly. Why, she's probably jealous of you."

"Of *me?*"

"Sure... because you're going to be a mother soon, and you have a devoted, sensational husband."

"Oh, I don't know," Kate said. "I can remember me, five years ago. There was a married woman with two small kids living next door, and each time I hopped out on a big date and saw her behind the kitchen window, I felt a positive compassion. I wouldn't have changed places with her for anything. To me, she was already a has-been."

She caught sight of herself in a mirror nearby and was silent. Despite the fact that she had recently washed her hair, it fell in spaghetti-like strands; her skin had a dull look. She thought: I hope all my shine and bloom is going down to the baby.

"I wish veils would come back," she said, looking hopefully at Joe.

"Oh, you're not so bad," he teased.

She felt exasperated. "You're supposed to say I have The True Inner Glow of Motherhood at this stage!"

He straightened his glasses. "You do have an inner glow," he said. "I only hope it's not heartburn, like last night."

"Oh, you." But she was grinning as she flopped down beside him. He put his arm around her and pressed his cheek against her hair. They sat like that for a while, close, content. Then he murmured, "Did you take your calcium pill?"

She nodded. Suddenly an image flared in her mind; she saw Miss Ilona Graham sitting beside a swinging young man who was asking her in a deep, caressing voice, "Did you take your calcium pill?"

She wanted to laugh. But she didn't. Somehow the little joke held a faint sting, she didn't know why.

One evening she and Joe left the apartment to go out. In the hall, the girl from 17C was standing with a sensational young man; the elevator was just arriving. They all entered and stood motionless as it started down.

Kate stole a glance at the girl. She was wearing a revealing slither of white silk, and even her skin, Kate thought admiringly, looked expensive. She shifted her gaze. The elevator had corner mirrors and she saw Joe's face framed in one. He was staring in the same direction she had been a moment before.

She had a sense of shock. Not only was there admiration in his face but something else — a wistfulness, a yearning. Even — a wanting? She glanced away quickly.

Later, walking up the street with Joe, the twist of jealousy still sharp inside her, she said, "Miss Ilona Graham adds tone to the elevator."

"She sure does," Joe said.

They walked on. A pinched look had come to her mouth.

Yet, in the days that followed, she told herself that she had been crazy. Joe was the same man she had fallen in love with so deeply five years before — a man of charm and wit, attentive, his suits always slightly rumpled, his ties a little askew. But his eyes, behind the glasses that were never quite straight on his nose, were the eyes of a man to be trusted.

Still — a slight unease persisted. She began to take extra pains with her appearance, although at this stage of her pregnancy, she thought bleakly, it was about as effective as applying false eyelashes to a whale. Each night, she refused to relinquish the bag of garbage to her husband, claiming that she wanted to stretch her legs. Why take chances on his meeting the dazzling Miss Graham — at the incinerator? How idiotic it was! she admitted sheepishly to herself.

But as time passed, another meeting was unavoidable. It happened at the end of an evening out when they were waiting in the lobby for the elevator. The girl and a very attractive young man appeared at their side; they all entered the elevator when it came and then faced forward as it began its long ascent.

Kate stood stiffly. I won't look at Joe, she thought. She was suddenly terribly conscious of her body; it seemed to her that it was growing bigger, bigger and more grotesque, until it threatened to squash the other three against the walls, like something in a science-fiction movie. The floors were flashing their numbers above 12, 13, 14. As if pulled by an irresistible suction, her eyes went to the mirror opposite.

Anguish immediately pierced through her. For the look was on Joe's face again. There was no mistaking it.

Back in their bedroom minutes later, she was so sick at heart that she was unable to bear it. She turned to Joe, who was buttoning his pajamas. "I saw you looking across the elevator." Her voice was thick. "You were like a kid in front of a bakery window."

His fingers stopped; he blushed. "You see too much," he said.

"Well —" She gazed down, her eyes smarting. "The truth is the truth."

They were silent. Suddenly, he gave a rueful laugh. "I've always envied guys like that," he said.

Her head jerked up. "Guys?"

He sighed. "Those swinging men-about-town with their landscaped hair and their wide-striped shirts and their year-round tans." He shook his head. "They're so — so put together. Right on the nose. Cool. Real class." Admiration enriched his voice. "Why, you could take the one in the elevator tonight and put him behind the wheel of a $16,000 Italian racing car and he'd look perfect — as if he grew there."

She was stupefied. Finally she stammered, "B-but didn't you notice how gorgeous *she* was?"

He turned to her, surprised. "New York is filled with pretty girls. Half the time, I don't look twice." His expression changed, became respectful. "Now *you* I would look at twice." He coughed. "I'd have to look twice to get you all in."

Suddenly she felt good; she felt wonderful. "You know?" she said. "I think you'd look great behind the wheel of an Italian racing car."

"Ha." He rolled his eyes ceilingward and then looked at her again. "I think you have The True Inner Glow of Motherhood."

"Ha."

She went over and put her arms around his neck; his arms went to her shoulders; their cheeks touched. She whispered, "Come closer."

"I can't," he whispered back. "This is as close as I can get."

They both burst out laughing. And then their laughter faded and they just stood there, their eyes closed, holding each other awkwardly and off-balance, swaying gently.

A telephone rang beyond a wall; a radio was turned on somewhere; but she didn't hear a thing. And as the quiet, warm, sweet, floating moments passed, suddenly Kate didn't feel flat-footed or heavy or ungainly any more.

She felt like the most beautiful girl in the world.

Often in those years when the children are in school
and love has survived all the turmoil of its first
moments, life settles into a comfortable niche. However,
this need not be a static place, but rather like
a warm caress, somewhere we want to be. In the next
selections are some thoughts by famous writers on these
years when love is not just older — it is definitely better.

Poem in Prose

Archibald MacLeish

This poem is for my wife
I have made it plainly and honestly
The mark is on it
Like the burl on the knife

I have not made it for praise
She has no more need for praise
Than summer has
On the bright days

In all that becomes a woman
Her words and her ways are beautiful
Love's lovely duty
The well-swept room

Wherever she is there is sun
And time and a sweet air
Peace is there
Work done

There are always curtains and flowers
And candles and baked bread
And a cloth spread
And a clean house

Her voice when she sings is a voice
At dawn by a freshening sea
Where the wave leaps in the
Wind and rejoices

Wherever she is it is now
It is here where the apples are
Here in the stars
In the quick hour

The greatest and richest good —
My own life to live —
This she has given me

If giver could

Collar Holler

Janice Marshall

He's sweet and gentle
My loving spouse,
As he quietly paces
Throughout the house.
A broken water pipe,
Mice in the pool,
A spoon in the disposal,
He still keeps his cool.
But behold the hysterics
From this soft-spoken scholar,
Should I inadvertently starch
His button-down collar.

What Love Is

James Thurber

A lady of 47 who has been married 27 years and has six
children knows what love really is and once described
it for me like this:

"Love is what you've been through with somebody."

A Decade

Amy Lowell

When you came, you were like red wine and honey,
And the taste of you burnt my mouth with its sweetness.
Now you are like morning bread,
Smooth and pleasant.
I hardly taste you at all, for I know your savor;
But I am completely nourished.

Letter About Love
Paul Engle

Your hand is home. Whether in light or dark
Like friendly dogs your fingers leap and bark.
The sun comes from the east, wind from the south.
I come from silence to your talking mouth.
I come to search with you over the wild
Landscape of love, and not as a lost child,
Frantic for any touching, warm and human,
But as a man, praising you as a woman.

We talk. That is as useless as to sing.
Our slick words mock this marvelous, plain thing:
A man gives so that he may ask to live.
A woman's way of asking is to give.

Live stars need darkness to reveal their light,
But love, that is our doom and our delight,
Needs neither day nor dark, but only being
Together, in one presence, closer than seeing....

Well Met
Abbie Huston Evans

You are one of the few who matter, of those whom I count
On the fingers of one hand. I marvel how we live
Together in time. When I think how easy it is
To miss one man in the jungle of time, I quake
Thinking of those long-dead and of those unborn,
Sprinkled apart like stars in the dark, I cry, —
"Whoever else has been missed in the dark — the true,
The bright, the deep-to-be-loved — it has not been you!"

These Things
Gordon Parks

The way you draw the sun
         to sunless places,
The way your voice rings clear
         above mumbling voices —
These are things I love you for.

Your winsome pouting
About unimportant things,
The awful movies you adore,
The ear-sore songs you sing,
Your eyes smiling above the frowns —
You frown with such affection —
And the steamhot cloth
With which each evening
You rub from my face
The grime of city days —
These are things I love you for.

The way you find charm
         in charmless faces
And something of worth in a futile cause,
The way you take sides
         with luckless people —
These things and many more
Are all the things I love you for.

Love in the golden years "makes the lovely fires of youth pale beside its magnificence," writes Sylvia Gray. In this and other selections, love is shown to develop a depth and breadth that are only possible with experience and time.

from **The Art of Love**
Sylvia Gray

...The wonderful love of maturity makes the lovely
fires of youth pale beside its magnificence; its rich
and warmer glow; its fruits of experience which only
add charm and beauty to the mystery of love; its trust
in each other and the deeper understanding of intimate
and cherished moments which no sorrow can blot out;
even death itself cannot destroy this joyous soul
communion....

Buttercup Fields

Rob Wood

I remember our first summer...
  Buttercup fields
  And the scent of hay,
I remember evening falling...
  And walking hand in hand
  At the close of day.
Sunsets seemed so much more lovely
  Than sunsets
  Ever seemed before,
When you and I would walk together...
  In buttercup fields
  In the days of yore.
Somehow summer never left us...
  We saved its sunshine
  In our hearts
And never knew the chill of winter,
  For we shared the warmth
  That love imparts.
Thanks for all the joys of summer.
  More than that,
  What can I say?
Except that always I'll remember
  Buttercup fields
  And the scent of hay.

The secret to a happy marriage? Sometimes it's trying to say just the right thing or even saying nothing at all. As the following story shows, this kind of consideration goes a long way — maybe fifty years!

Speaking of Love

G. Groman

Mary Ann stood outside the door with an armload of bundles, waiting for Henry to answer the doorbell. The late morning sun glistened on the tidy gray braids on top of her head. The door swung open.

"Here, let me take those," Henry said, removing the packages from her arms as she came inside. "See!" He nodded his silver head toward the love seat. "I moved it while you were gone. You were right. It does look better over there." He forged on into the kitchen with the load.

Henry! She thought wryly, *I said the right side of the fireplace, not the left — where everybody at the party tonight will bump into it.* She walked purposefully toward the love seat, then stopped. *Henry had put it there. Besides, she didn't have time to change it — so much to do.*

"Honey," Henry's voice called from the kitchen, "did you see the flowers? They came an hour ago."

Spotting the yellow roses hanging precariously over the rim of the vase on the coffee table, she moved to rearrange them, as Henry continued, "I was very careful. Arranged them just like you do — all scraggled apart."

Mary Ann's hand stopped in mid-air.

"Now you won't have to trouble yourself about that," he said.

If she changed the arrangement, he'd notice. He was very sensitive about such things. Her hand dropped as she called back, "The roses are just beautiful, Henry."

*That wasn't a lie. How long they'd stay beautiful
drooping out of the water like that was a matter of
speculation. Maybe she could just poke one or two — .*
Her fingers stretched toward the roses. Then she heard
a scraping of feet just behind her. She spun around
with guilty haste.

"They're all right, aren't they?" Henry asked.

"Just lovely, Henry." She hurried on into the bedroom.
Slipping out of her shoes and unbuttoning her
blouse, she called back over her shoulder, "Do you mind
if we wait to have lunch until one o'clock?" *There
was just time to change her clothes. She would get
those two gray occasional chairs from the attic for
extra seating. The upholstery was a little worn — .*
"I have to get the extra gray chairs out of the attic,"
she called aloud to Henry, by way of apology. *She
always fixed a hot lunch, but maybe she could fix sandwiches —
just this once.*

"We can't have lunch that late, Mary Ann," Henry's
voice floated up the hall.

She stood rigid in front of the bedroom mirror.

"Why not, Henry?"

"Because — " There was a thumping noise, and his
voice faded away entirely, then came back muffled.
"The reporter is — " another thud, and the voice clearer.
"Coming — uh — " *Was he moving something?* "Coming at
noon." His voice became normal.

"What are you doing?"

"Just helping. Don't you remember, honey? About
the reporter, I mean. You said to have him come at
noon if he could. Oh, we're big celebrities today,
Mary Ann."

*No. She hadn't said noon. She'd said any time but
noon. She shrugged. Well, noon wasn't all that
inconvenient. How long could it take to ask a few questions
and snap a picture? The party wasn't till seven.*

"That reporter seemed like a nice young fella,"
Henry's voice bubbled with enthusiasm. "I told him,
since it was noon, maybe he'd like to stay for lunch.
Told him you're the best cook in the world, and we
always have a hot meal."

A hot lunch! Henry, you didn't!

"Told him about your biscuits, too." Henry appeared
at the door. "How you make biscuits that just melt in
your mouth, and you can whip them up in no time. He
said it was years since he'd had a decent biscuit."

*Now what? Should she change to a housedress, then
back again for the pictures? Or would he want to take
pictures first? The dress she had on was much too nice
for kitchen work.* She turned and smiled.

"Henry. You're always telling people about my biscuits.
Looks like you'd be tired of them after all these years."

He looked pleased and leaned against the door frame.

"Man called from the bakery about the icing for the
cake. Asked if you wanted banana or orange. I told
him. Cake'll be here at five."

*The icing! Not banana! Henry, you remember your
best friend breaks out in hives any time he goes near
anything like a banana.*

"Which one did you tell him, Henry?"

"Oh, don't worry. I remembered."

"Good." She started back to the living room.

"Told him it had to be banana, because everything is
supposed to be gold — not orange." He trailed just
behind her, until she stepped through the doorway, when
he moved around in front. "Surprise!" he gestured
with an open palm. "I did it while you were fixing
your hair in there."

Mary Ann gasped. *Where on earth had all these ugly
gray folding chairs come from? Oh, yes. The funeral
home that went out of business fifteen years ago, and
at the auction those twenty chairs —. The sign was*

still on the back, 'Property of McNaughton Funeral Home.'

"You did say you wanted them out of the attic."

"You're very thoughtful, Henry."

Henry's eyes crinkled at the corners. "Want me to set the table for lunch?"

"No, thanks. I'll take care of it. Just go on outside and rest. You've been working all morning."

An hour later, the reporter was sitting at the kitchen table with the remnants of the hot meal on his empty plate. Reaching over to close his hand around Mary Ann's, he grinned. "Delicious. If I could find a girl like you, I'd want to be married for fifty years, too. Is that the secret of your happy marriage?"

"No," Henry's head gave a quick shake. "She couldn't cook at all when we were first married. It was her sweet nature that kept this marriage young. The first few years were a bit rough; but after that, never a cross word."

Mary Ann looked through the kitchen door at the love seat; at the partially wilted roses; at the gray chairs lining the wall; her eyes traveled to the lone remaining biscuit on the kitchen table, as her hands smoothed at the wrinkles in her dress.

I never say a cross word, she thought, *because I love you, Henry.*

They were standing at the door a few minutes later, waving good-bye to the reporter, before Mary Ann spoke to her husband again.

"Henry."

"M-m-m."

"You didn't ever say I was a bad cook when we were first married."

"No."

"Why not?"

"It didn't seem important. Silence can be golden, you know."

How Can I Grow Old?

Reginald Holmes

How can I grow old,
    with a winter moon shining
And casting its shadows
    on new-fallen snow?
The heavens aglow,
    all the stars shining brightly;
How can I grow old,
    when I'm loving you so?

For a Wedding Anniversary

Roselle Mercier Montgomery

Companioned years have made them comprehend
The comradeship that lies beyond a kiss.
The young ask much of life — they ask but this,
To fare the road together to its end.

True Love

James Russell Lowell

True love is but a humble, lowborn thing, And hath its
food served up in earthen ware; it is a thing to walk
with, hand in hand, through the every dayness of this
workday world, Baring its tender feet to every flint.
Yet letting not one heart-beat go astray From Beauty's
law of plainness and content; A simple, fireside thing,
whose quiet smile Can warm earth's poorest hovel to a
home; Which, when our autumn cometh, as it must, And
life in the chill wind shivers bare and leafless, Shall
still be blest with Indian-summer youth In bleak November,
and, with thankful heart, Smile on its sample
stores of garnered fruit, As full of sunshine to our
aged eyes As when it nursed the blossoms of our spring.

Love Is a Funny Thing

Thomas Malloy

Love is a funny thing.
  Revealing!
And marriage exposes each flaw
  you're concealing.
It lets you hear snores,
lets you see every wart,
but still it can show you
the depths of a heart.
Love is a growing thing.

Love is a funny thing.
  For two!
Then all of a sudden,
there's somebody new,
somebody hungry and angry
  and screaming,
someone you love
with a joy beyond dreaming.
Love is a tender thing.

Love is a funny thing.
  A riot!
You're both past your prime
and in need of a diet.
But once in a while,
all alone, there's a look
that puts down the knitting
and closes the book.
Love is the only thing.

Some loves last fifty years, some only a week. But however long, each love teaches us something about ourselves and others, and helps us to move on to either a deeper kind of love or to a new one. What really matters is that love is always there — always with us — filling up every moment of our lives.

The Colors of Love
Ruth A. Jacob

New love is pink, blush.
The whole world looks bright
When seen through
The rose glow of delight.

Love is orange-yellow,
Warm as the sun,
Radiant, vital,
When two are as one.

Blue is regret
For the words left unspoken,
Kindness forgotten,
Promises broken.

Pure white is the love
That comforts, that cares,
Forgetful of self,
All burdens bears.

Gold are the memories,
Golden the laughter,
Golden forgiveness
And grace ever after.

Happiness, sadness,
Peacefulness, strife —
The colors of love
Are the colors of life.

For Those Who Love

Henry van Dyke

Time is...
    Too slow for those who wait,
Too swift for those who fear,
    Too long for those who grieve,
        Too short for those who rejoice;
But for those who love,
        Time is not.

dear   nancy,

    let time go lightly...

            love gary.